Resilience vs Surviving

Marc Royster-Stallion

For personal orders, catalogs, or other information, write to
kevin@ibmg365.com or assist.stallion@gmail.com

Books may be purchased or special orders/readings can be organized by contacting the publisher, author or management at: kevin@ibmg365.com or (818) 469-5863
Cover Design: Aurelie A. Royster
Cover Art: Woman/Canva
LuLu Publishing Services
Publisher: Marcus Royster (Marc Royster-Stallion)
ISBN: 978-1-387-26176-5 | Ebook Edition
[1. Personal Growth— Self Help 2. Spirituality 3. Religion 4. Psychology 5. Book One— Pocket Book Edition]

I would like to introduce you to the Pocket Coach Series. This series is designed to challenge your perspective and act as an active coach that you can carry with you at all times. Having a coach in today's time is imperative to progress. As a coach, it's my goal to help you realize that you are the expert at your own life. I am here to simply offer tools and challenge your perspective, so that you may begin to develop a more holistic approach to life.

It's very easy to become consumed by our everyday problems, tasks, and obligations. When we are focused on the *urgent things*, by nature we neglect the *important things*. It's the coach's job to keep you focused on the important tasks, despite the urgent matters surrounding you. That is the role of this series.

Your role is to receive, question, connect, and apply what we discover together. I will often start by exploring a concept in technical terms so that we may become more enlightened about what it is that we are actually analyzing.

I will then connect that concept to a relatable story, so that we can examine how that concept may play out in real life. These stories may be my own, from individuals that I may know, or very intriguing stories that I have learned over the years.

At the end of each book, I will offer a list of tools and exercises that you can begin to apply to your daily life immediately. These are tools that have been highly successful in my life, and the life of my clients.

Feel free to carry this book around with you. Use it as a reminder, as a guide, or as a motivation to make progressive change in your life. I hope that this experience is a progressive one, and one of many. Let's get started!

What if I told you that you are not who you think you are, and none of it is your fault?

Have you ever gotten the compliment, "Wow, you're so resilient, so brave!"? It probably made you feel as though you could face anything, or anyone. The feeling of "bouncing back", or "getting back up" after a stressful situation can be empowering, especially when you are recognized for it. The challenge is, identifying why you "bounced back" or "got back up". What was the driving force behind this "resilience"?

The purpose of this book is to help you identify a cognitive belief that may seem positive, but could actually be affecting your life negatively. Hopefully, after reading, and applying the exercises, you'll be able to start taking actionable steps.

COGNITIVE BELIEF

What is a Cognitive Belief? Well, belief is summarized as the cognitive act or state in which a proposition is taken to be true. Belief is a propositional attitude; it can be a subjective probability.

We all have our own beliefs, some positive and others negative. An example of a negative cognitive belief is "I am unlovable", or "It's impossible for me to learn new skills", a very popular one is "I'll never be good enough". Let us not confuse belief as an emotion. The beliefs can certainly lead to particular emotions, which then leads to a variety of behaviors. These beliefs can, and often do lead to destructive behaviors.

For example, a woman that suffers from violence, physical and mental abuse may start to believe that she deserves the treatment.

On the other end, the abuser may have beliefs that if he doesn't show force, he will not receive love. He could also believe that violence is a way of showing and retaining love. All beliefs (positive or negative) affect our behaviors. An example of a positive belief that may affect our behavior is a spiritual or religious belief.

These kinds of beliefs influence our rituals and daily routines. Some beliefs are as simple as "breakfast is the most important meal of the day". We were told this by our parents and they were told this by their parents and so forth, but is this true? How many of us have taken the time to research and vet this belief?

Maybe, most of us are afraid to debunk some beliefs that we may have. This would mean change, and of course, change is scary (we will revisit this later). Now that we have a basic understanding of what a cognitive belief is, let us examine this idea of being resilient.

RESILIENCE

The textbook definition says "the capacity to recover quickly from difficulties; toughness." and "the ability of a substance or object to spring back into shape; elasticity". In my opinion, the term has become such a buzz word, and the definition doesn't reflect an accurate depiction of real-life application. There is value to be had in clarifying exactly what resilience is.

Some have even argued that resilience is an "empty concept", but I trust that resilience has a lot to do with change. The concept of resilience is fairly new believe it or not. According to Ann Masten, a professor at the University of Minnesota College of Education and Human Development, "the idea of resilience emerged in ecology and psychology, or the social sciences... around the 1970's". This concept happened independently.

The way that Masten defines resilience is "[t]he capacity of a dynamic system to adapt successfully to challenges that threaten the function, survival, or future development of the system".

This definition suggests that resilience is desirable. However, some things can be persistent and "resilient" but not desirable. For example, poverty is somehow resilient, yet it is undesirable, right?

This idea came from ecology. An ecologist named C.S. (Buzz) Holling defined resilience as "a measure of the persistence of systems and their ability to absorb change and disturbance and still maintain the same relationships between populations or state variables". He was trying to figure out why or how something could be disturbed, yet avoid moving into a different state.

For example, if I add food coloring into a glass of water, the water will persist, it may be red, blue or green, yet the water is resilient enough to keep its state.

We will revisit this later because both, Holling and Masten define something really important.

The truth is, we all face challenges in life. Sometimes, they come as small inconveniences, other times they come as aggressive waves, sucking us in, and pushing us back. The pressures can be overwhelming and sometimes disabling. But somehow, we keep going. No matter how hard it is, we find ourselves waking up and slugging to work, school, or wherever it is that we need to be.

Others who may not be facing the same difficult challenges at the moment, look at us and think "Wow, they are so resilient!".

Having lived in Haiti now for a year, I've heard it almost non-stop. "Haiti is such a resilient country", or "That country has been through hell, they are so resilient". I've even listened to locals talk about how "resilient the Haitien people are".

I love Haiti, and I share pride in their culture and history. Ever since moving here, I've felt a deep spiritual connection to the land and the people. However, every time that I hear *Haiti* and *resilience* in the same sentence, I get an awkward feeling in my stomach. In fact, this feeling is what has inspired me to write this pocket book.

SURVIVING

Now that we have examined resilience a little bit, let's look at the concept of surviving or survival. If we look in the dictionary we'll see, "remaining alive", or "continuing to exist; remaining intact".

The Webster dictionary words it in an interesting manner, "still living after another or others have died or died out". I say interesting, because most of the definitions out there suggest a concept of "remaining", or "existing" not "living".

Most of us share a positive connotation for the word "living". For most of us, living surpasses surviving. We want to "live our best life" not "survive our best life" right? Depending on the situation, surviving can have a negative connotation.

The immediate goal for most individuals living in poverty is to survive. The idea of living is usually suppressed by constant pressures, fears, and doubts.

Growing up, I watched my mother struggle to provide for me and my five siblings alone. Sometimes, she'd be working two jobs and have to decide whether she should pay the power bill or grocery shop. If she chose to buy food, everything had to be meals that could be prepared without power, because the next day the lights would be out. A lot of the times the food that we ate had nothing to do with our desired tastes and favorite meals, which would have been a glimpse of living. What we ate was a condition of survival.

Our habits and behaviors are derived from our instincts. If I were to ask my mother "why", she'd respond "Because I had no choice", "I had to keep a roof over your head", "I had to protect you". All of these responses are influenced by a survivor's mentality.

RESILIENCE vs SURVIVING

A woman once said to me "your mother must be proud, her resilience has paid off in you". At first this sounded very good. But, after a while it hit me... my mother is an expert survivor, she hasn't had the chance to be resilient.

Like the definition from ecologist, C.S. (Buzz) Holling, my mother was good at maintaining her state while absorbing change and disturbance. She continued to bounce back. I've always seen my mother as a "strong, black woman" which she has proven time and time again.

Like most species and creatures here on earth, she has become this by nature. Because in order to survive, she has had to adapt and readapt to the pressures around her.

Here is an easy way to think about it: Resilience is conscious, one must choose this desired route to not only overcome a circumstance, but to surpass it and progress forward. "Bouncing back" is NOT a goal.

Surviving on the other hand is chance and instincts. You survive a situation that others could not because you were in the right place at the right time, or because you had no other choice besides death or despair. Your instincts kicked in and said "get back up, you can't die here". In surviving, you do not necessarily overcome the pressure or stress of the circumstance, instead you learn to live with it because you have to.

After self-assessing and making conscious decisions to progress, my mother is no longer just a strong black woman, she becomes a resilient black woman that uses unfortunate circumstances to her advantage.

This is where that feeling in my stomach comes from when Haiti is described as a resilient country. I would love for that to be true, because then Haiti would become the fascinating and magical country that we all know it could be. The history of Haiti is indeed a resilient one. The first black nation to fight for and claim its freedom to break from colonization is a resilient trait. But, since then, Haiti has been burdened with the pressures of survival. Not only has democracy been in an upward hill battle for survival, but the people of Haiti have struggled to make a conscious and deliberate effort to live and progress. The insecurities and unstable safety have influenced the citizens to stick to the basic needs of survival.

The devastating earthquake of 2010 has set Haiti back. Some would argue that Haiti has hardly "bounced back" at all. This most recent 2021 earthquake has reminded Haiti that conscious retaliation is mandatory if we want to see progress in the country.

What would this look like? This would look like interventions in the modeling and structuring of homes and buildings. The Government would mandate a new safety and building code suitable for earthquakes. The Government would better regulate taxes to allocate funds to a bigger more efficient disaster relief budget. Bigger shelters would be built for displaced families and individuals. I do not know all of the answers, but I do know that these types of intentional decisions would lead to a more resilient future. Remember how Masten describes resilience? "The capacity... to adapt successfully to challenges that threaten the function, survival, or future development".

I believe that once intentional progress has been accomplished as a result of the negative circumstance, resilience has been achieved. Until a conscious shift has happened and acted as the catalyst for change, one remains a survivor. Positive change is the result that we are looking for. This is why "bouncing back" belongs under the umbrella of survival, and not resilience.

WHAT AM I?

Unfortunately, you may have been waking up with the belief that you are resilient because you haven't given up. After evaluating, you may realize that you are a survivor that has yet to reach true resilience. This is okay, because the good news is, it is never too late to become resilient.

Follow these steps to self-evaluation and reflect. Once an honest assessment has happened, you can then apply the practice to achieving resilience.

Do an honest evaluation on yourself: *(Answer each question truthfully and wholeheartedly) These questions are just to provoke you to think. There is no exact science.*

1.   When I continue going through the motions, am I consciously deciding to keep going or am I acting out of instincts for survival?

Scenario example: If you were starving, and on your way to purchase food, but a thief robbed you, leaving you with no money, would your first reaction be about:

A.   The hunger
B.   Future prevention

If you chose A, then you have a survivor's mentality and not a resilient one. You are concerned with the immediate need to remain, opposed to the need to progress.

2.   When I continue through the motions am I progressing, or just bouncing-back?

Scenario example: You are bullied about the freckles on your face, the curls in your hair, or the pimples on your face. Do you:

A.   Publicly embrace your features.
B.   Learn to take an insult and keep it moving.

If you chose B, then you have a survivor's mentality and not a resilient one. You are concerned with getting through, and dealing with the bullying, opposed to embracing and celebrating your features.

3.   The last time I was faced with pressure or a difficult situation, did I just deal with it or did I consciously progress from it?

Scenario example: You were faced with overwhelming pressure, stress and anxiety; however, you found a way through. Once on the other side, did you notice that:

A.   You were positively changed as a result of your struggle, and you intentionally allowed that change to affect your life somehow.

B.   You are still the same, with more experience and wisdom, but nothing life changing has necessarily happened.

If you chose B, then at that moment you were surviving and not being resilient. You have bounced back from the situation, but you haven't allowed the circumstances to change you for the better.

A good question to ask yourself is: "Do I look for a way out or a way through?". If you look for a way through, then you know that there is something inside of that struggle that you can take with you to enhance your life; that is resilience.

Ask yourself: "Does life happen **to** me or **for** me? If you honestly believe that life happens for you, then you have a resilient mindset.

My first time being aware of my resilience was in high school. It was a normal day; I was passing between classes as the bells rang. I was what they called C lunch, meaning I was with a group of students that ate lunch 3rd in the day. I remember the bell rang for lunch and my phone began to ring simultaneously. *Ding* after *Ding,* when I finally looked at my phone, I had received several messages from my mother: "Where are you?", "COME

HOME NOW!", "Hurry up and GET HERE!". Of course, I was alarmed and frightened, it was the middle of a school day and she's telling me to leave school to get home.

I quickly snuck out of school from one of the side exits. During my ten-minute walk home, all sorts of thoughts danced around my head. Someone died. Your sister was found shot. Someone is going to prison. There is a fire at the house. We won thirty million dollars from the lottery. I was so nervous that I stopped to throw up, but nothing came out but sound.

When I finally arrived, I saw my mom's car full of things. There were a few Caucasian individuals standing in front of the house with blank expressions. My mother came racing from the front door with bags in her arms, "Go grab all of your things, hurry up! These bastards are taking the house from us!". My stomach sank to the floor. I remember making eye contact with one of the women standing there. I was searching for empathy, a sense of sadness or regret, but I got nothing. Her face remained motionless. After racing around for several minutes trying to grab all of our important things, I realized that I had to go back to school. My mother and sister's car were too full to fit me.

On the way back to school I contemplated several things. I thought about running away. Maybe just not going back to school. I imagined going to the gas station, playing the lottery and winning instantly. I would go to the bank, cash my winnings and pay my mom's house off with cash money. I even thought about turning around and setting a fire in the house. By the time I made it to school grounds I hadn't decided anything. I remember walking inside of the building and realizing that lunch had yet to end. All of that happened in less than an hour, but for me, it felt like days had passed.

This has to have been one of the biggest shocks of my life. Everyone was acting so normal. My friends were running around joking and laughing as if the world wasn't on fire. No one seemed to be worried about anything.

Before I knew it, the bell had rung and the halls quickly filled up. For me everything was moving so slow, but the heart inside of my chest was pounding like the hooves of a race horse. I remember trying to be one of the first in class so that I could have a moment to myself. I walked in, sat at my desk and put my head down. One of my friends, *Georgia,* walks past my desk and utters "one of those days?". The bell rings. My teacher quickly moves around the room placing tests on everyone's desks. Immediately, my entire body goes hot. My first thought is to scream... as loud as I can.

My next thought is to stand up, rip the test and throw it on the teacher's desk. My body felt like it was in a constant glitch. I wanted to jump up, but something kept holding me down. The feeling was sickening. How could she give me a test, when I don't have a home to go to? How could I focus on something so conditional, when my physical world was shattering before me. School automatically became irrelevant.

It meant nothing to me anymore. At that moment I was alone in a world that hated me and everything going on was to punish me. See, I had the cognitive belief that life was happening to me.

As soon as I had built enough courage to stand up, it felt like I had ten thoughts for every step that I took towards her desk: "Are you really going to do this?", "Is that all it takes to stop you", "Will ripping this test bring your house back", "Will dropping out of school ease your pain", "will this help your mom build another home?". I was riddled with questions. When I finally made it to her desk, she looked up at me with her big owl-like eyes and her orange, burnt rusted hair. "Yes?" she said. Before I could cry, I asked "can I run to the bathroom?". She took my test and said "Take the pass". When I made it to the restroom, I began to cry. It was like a projectile vomit from my eyes. All of that stress and anger rushed out of me. I thought it was because of the pain that I was feeling. But it was actually because I had made the decision to never let this happen again. The decision to take what has happened and wield it as a sword to fight for my future was freeing.

I didn't know at the time that this was resilience, but the freedom that I felt in the moment was so overwhelming that I had no choice but to let it out. That moment has defined who I have become and what I've been capable of. After that day, I made a conscious decision to never let anyone tell me that I "can't have" something. I asked myself a million times, "what can I have, what can I possess, that no one can take from me?". The answer was resilience. No one can take my ability to consciously grow from unfortunate circumstances.

Remember the purpose of this book, I want to help you identify a cognitive belief that may seem positive, but could actually be affecting your life negatively. That belief is "I am resilient". After evaluating yourself, did you find yourself to be more of a survivor than resilient? If so, now is the time to consciously make a shift in your habits. You have the power to become resilient. It brings a new type of freedom that enables us to move beyond adaptability. Resilience isn't the wings that take us through the air, it is the air itself that carries the wings. It doesn't exist because it has to, it exists because it wants to. It is fully conscious.

PRACTICE RESILIENCE

☐ First admit to yourself that you are a survivor and from this day forward you will achieve resilience.

☐ Write down 3-5 beliefs that you have about yourself that you are unwilling to change. Circle the ones that have been challenged in life. How did you feel when those beliefs were under pressure? This will help you reflect on why certain beliefs are important to you.

☐ When faced with a difficult challenge, ask yourself, "How can I use this to my advantage?"

☐ The next time you feel overwhelmed, ask yourself, "Am I overwhelmed because I am trying to bear the weight of my challenges and am unwilling to change?"

☐ When faced with pressure, take a second to write down three things that could possibly be a positive outcome of your situation, if you intentionally act upon it.

☐ Write down five stressful events or circumstances that have happened in your life. Put a check mark next to each thing that you have intentionally used to better your life, and circle each thing that has just passed and nothing positive has happened as a result. Next to each situation that you have circled, write 1-2 ways that you could intentionally use that situation to progress your life.

- [ ] Ask yourself, am I willing to change? If the answer is no, write yourself a short letter explaining why you are unwilling to change.

- [ ] The next time you feel like giving up, write down your emotions and thoughts in the moment. Then ask yourself, "what is the possible reward for not giving up?".

- [ ] Be aware that actively taking a break is not the same as giving up. Sometimes we need a true moment to reflect and breathe. As long as you are proactive about this break, you are not giving up.

- [ ] Ask yourself, "Do I want to be resilient?". You must want it, it cannot just happen for you, otherwise you will begin to have a false narrative in your head, which can hinder rather than help you.

Try to incorporate these tools and questions into your daily habits. Try to make conscious decisions to be resilient. Remember that *progressive change* is the goal of resilience.

As cliché as it sounds, there isn't anything that you cannot do. As long as you are willing to shift your perspective, go through some uncomfortable pressures, and make a conscious decision to keep going, you will forever be unstoppable!

www.ingramcontent.com/pod-product-compliance
Lightning Source LLC
Chambersburg PA
CBHW071320280526
45788CB00004B/1956